the source

arrangements for worship groups

book 4

C instruments

arranged by Chris Mitchell

Kevin Mayhew

We hope you enjoy the music in this book.
Further copies of this and the other books in the series are available
from your local music shop or Christian bookshop.

In case of difficulty, please contact the publisher direct:

The Sales Department
KEVIN MAYHEW LTD
Rattlesden
Bury St Edmunds
Suffolk IP30 0SZ

Phone 01449 737978
Fax 01449 737834
E-mail info@kevinmayhewltd.com

Please ask for our complete catalogue of outstanding Church Music.

First published in Great Britain in 1998 by Kevin Mayhew Ltd.

© Copyright 1998 Kevin Mayhew Ltd.

ISBN 1 84003 125 5
ISMN M 57004 208 1
Catalogue No: 1470304
0 1 2 3 4 5 6 7 8 9

The music in this book is protected by copyright and may not be reproduced in
any way for sale or private use without the consent of the copyright owner.

Cover designed by Jaquetta Sergeant

Music arrangements by Chris Mitchell

Music setting by Chris Mitchell and Lynwen Davies

Printed and bound in Great Britain by
Caligraving Limited Thetford Norfolk

Contents

This index gives the first line of each hymn. If a hymn is known by an alternative title, this is also given, but indented and in italics.

	No.		No.
And his love goes on and on	325	Lord, have mercy	328
A living sacrifice	351	Lord, I come to you	329
All the glory	363	Lord, I lift your name on high	330
Amazing love	370	Lord, my heart cries out	331
Father me	382	Lord of lords	332
Firm foundation	302	Lord of the heavens	333
Glory to the King	331	*Lord of the years*	327
Great love	364	Lord, prepare me	334
Have faith in God	400	Lord, the light of your love	335
Heal our nation	337	Lord, we lift you high	336
Heaven is in my heart	388	Lord, we long for you	337
How great thou art	396	Lord, we long to see your glory	338
How majestic	395	Lord, you are more precious	339
I was made for this	389	Lord, you are so precious to me	340
Jesus, what a beautiful name	301	Lord, you have my heart	341
Jesus, you're my firm foundation	302	Lord, you put a tongue in my mouth	342
Jesus, your loving kindness	303	Love divine, all loves excelling	343
Jesus, your name is power	304	Love of Christ, come now	344
Joy to the world	305	Low in the grave he lay	345
Just as I am, without one plea	306	Majesty	346
King of kings and Lord of lords	307	Make a joyful noise, all ye people	347
King of kings	308	Make me a channel of your peace	348
King of kings, majesty	309	Make way, make way	349
Lamb of God	310	Man of sorrows	350
Lead us, heavenly Father, lead us	311	May our worship be as fragrance	351
Led like a lamb	312	May the fragrance	352
Let it be to me	313	Meekness and majesty	353
Let it rain	314	Men of faith	354
Let me be a sacrifice	315	Mercy is falling	355
Let the righteous sing	316	Mighty God	356
Let there be love	317	Mighty is our God	357
Let your living water flow	318	More about Jesus	358
Let your love come down	319	More love, more power	359
Let your word go forth	320	More of your glory	360
Lift up your heads	321	More than oxygen	361
Like a candle flame	322	My first love	362
Like a child	362	My heart is full	363
Living under the shadow of his wing	323	My heart will sing to you	364
Living water	318	My hope is built	365
Lo, he comes with clouds descending	324	My Jesus, I love thee	366
Look what God has done	325	My Jesus, my Saviour	367
Look what the Lord has done	326	My life is in you, Lord	368
Lord, for the years	327	My lips shall praise you	369

	No.		No.
My Lord, what love is this	370	O Lord, my heart is not proud	397
My Spirit rests in you	371	O Lord our God	398
Nearer, my God, to thee	372	O Lord, the clouds are gathering	399
No one but you, Lord	373	O Lord, you lead me	400
No other name	374	*O you gates*	321
No scenes of stately majesty	375	*Only you*	373
Not by might	376	*Power of your love*	329
Nothing shall separate us	377	*Prayer song*	328
Now unto the King	378	*Restorer of my soul*	369
O Breath of Life	379	*Sanctuary*	334
O come, all ye faithful	380	*Send the fire*	386
O come and join the dance	381	*Shadow of your wings*	371
O Father of the fatherless	382	*Shine, Jesus, shine*	335
O for a thousand tongues to sing	383	*Shout to the Lord*	367
O give thanks	384	*Shout to the North*	354
O God, most high	385	*Spirit song*	392
O God of burning, cleansing flame	386	*The candle song*	322
O happy day	387	*The King of glory comes*	308
O, heaven is in my heart	388	*The solid rock*	365
Oh, I was made for this	389	*This is your God*	353
Oh, lead me	390	*Unto the King*	378
O Jesus, I have promised	391	*We will magnify*	398
O let the Son of God enfold you	392	*Worship the Lord*	347
O little town of Bethlehem	393	*You came from heaven to earth*	330
O Lord, hear my prayer	394	*You have broken the chains*	385
O Lord, how majestic is your name	395	*Your love*	303
O Lord, my God	396	*You're alive*	312

CHRIS MITCHELL is a well-established arranger, composer, musical director and session musician who has worked with Graham Kendrick, David Peacock, Gloria Gaynor and the BBC. He and his wife, Linda, are experienced worship leaders and are involved in providing seminars and workshops for Christians in the arts.

the source will be developed into a major resource for the churches. It is already available in the following editions

Words Only	ISBN	1 84003 121 2
	Catalogue No.	1470101
Full Music	ISBN	1 84003 120 4
	ISMN	M 57004 204 3
	Catalogue No.	1470104
Complete Acetate Masters	ISBN	1 84003 119 0
	Catalogue No.	1470201

Arrangements for Worship Groups:

Book 1 for C instruments	ISBN	1 84003 122 0
	ISMN	M 57004 205 0
	Catalogue No.	1470301
Book 1 for B♭ instruments	ISBN	1 84003 128 X
	ISMN	M 57004 211 1
	Catalogue No.	1470307
Book 2 for C instruments	ISBN	1 84003 123 9
	ISMN	M 57004 206 7
	Catalogue No.	1470302
Book 2 for B♭ instruments	ISBN	1 84003 129 8
	ISMN	M 57004 212 8
	Catalogue No.	1470308
Book 3 for C instruments	ISBN	1 84003 124 7
	ISMN	M 57004 207 4
	Catalogue No.	1470303
Book 3 for B♭ instruments	ISBN	1 84003 130 1
	ISMN	M 57004 213 5
	Catalogue No.	1470309
Book 4 for C instruments	ISBN	1 84003 125 5
	ISMN	M 57004 208 1
	Catalogue No.	1470304
Book 4 for B♭ instruments	ISBN	1 84003 131 X
	ISMN	M 57004 214 2
	Catalogue No.	1470310

301 Jesus, what a beautiful name
Tanya Richards

3 verses

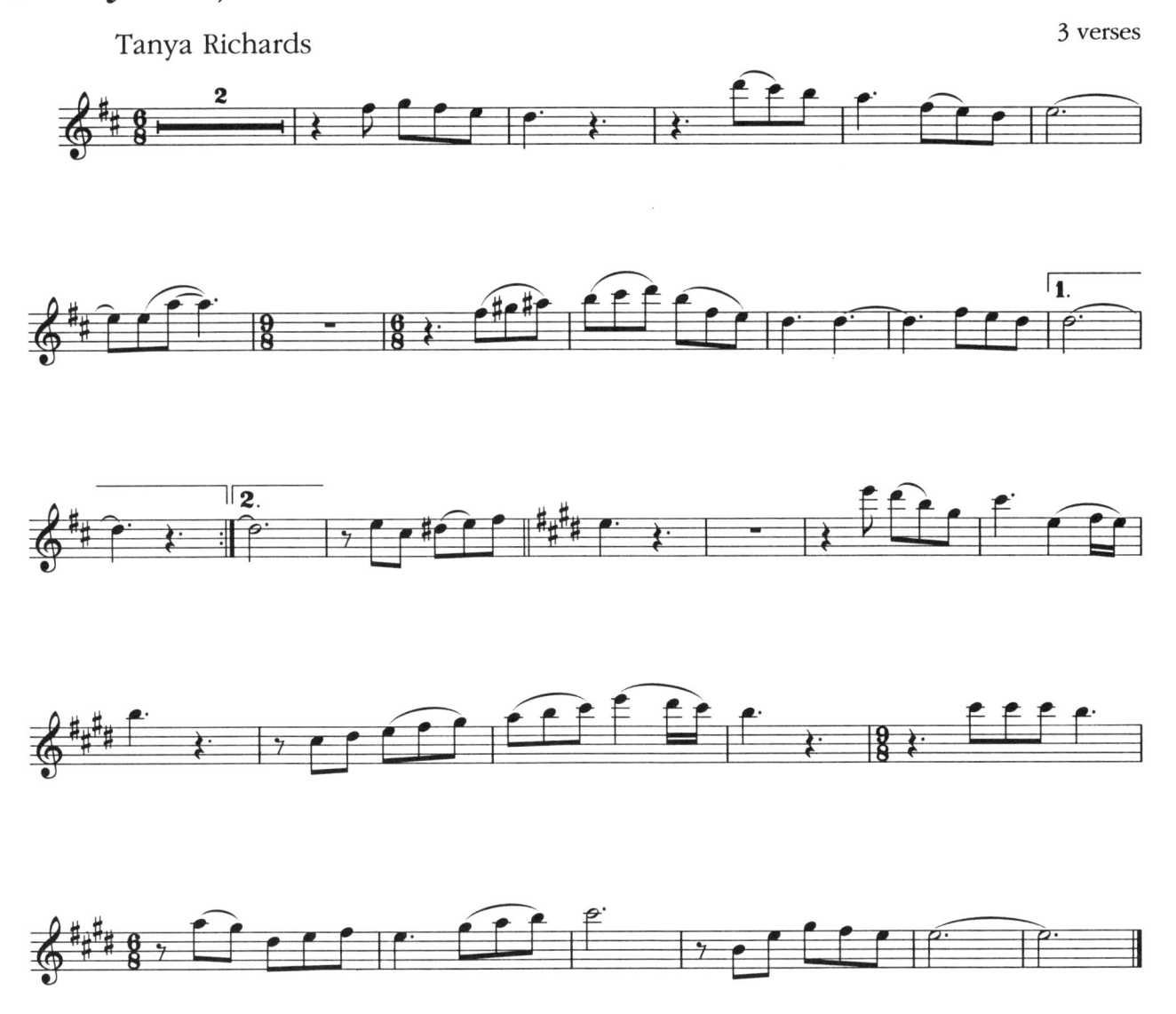

© Copyright 1995 Tanya Riches/Hillsongs Australia. Administered by Kingsway's
Thankyou Music, P.O. Box 75, Eastbourne, East Sussex, BN23 6NW, UK. Used by permission.

302 Jesus, you're my firm foundation
(Firm Foundation)
Nancy Gordon and Jamie Harvill

2 verses

© Copyright 1994 Integrity's Hosanna! Music/Integrity Praise! Administered by Kingsway's
Thankyou Music, P.O. Box 75, Eastbourne, East Sussex, BN23 6NW, UK. Used by permission.

303 Jesus, your loving kindness
(Your love)

Reuben Morgan

© Copyright 1996 Reuben Morgan/Hillsongs Australia. Administered by Kingsway's Thankyou Music, P.O. Box 75, Eastbourne, East Sussex, BN23 6NW, UK. Used by permission.

304 Jesus, your name is power

Morris Chapman

4 verses

Freely, with feeling

© Copyright 1992 Maranatha! Music/Word Music. Administered by CopyCare,
P.O. Box 77, Hailsham, East Sussex, BN27 3EF, UK. Used by permission.

305 Joy to the world

George Frideric Handel

3 verses

306 Just as I am, without one plea (Tune 1)

Henry Smart

6 verses

306a Just as I am, without one plea (Tune 2)

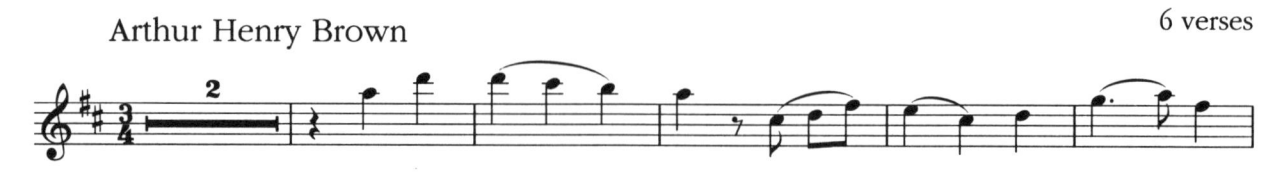

Arthur Henry Brown

6 verses

307 King of kings and Lord of lords

Naomi Batya and Sophie Conty

May be sung as a 2-part round

optional ending

© Copyright 1980 Maranatha! Music. Administered by CopyCare,
P.O. Box 77, Hailsham, East Sussex, BN27 3EF, UK. Used by permission.

308 King of kings
(The King of glory comes)

Graham Kendrick

Strongly

© Copyright 1988 Make Way Music, P.O. Box 263, Croydon, Surrey, CR9 5AP, UK.
International copyright secured. All rights reserved. Used by permission.

309 King of kings, majesty

Jarrod Cooper

2 verses

© Copyright 1996 Jarrod Cooper. Used by permission.

310 Lamb of God

Chris Bowater

© Copyright 1988 Sovereign Lifestyle Music Ltd, P.O. Box 356,
Leighton Buzzard, Bedfordshire, LU7 8WP, UK. Used by permission.

311 Lead us, heavenly Father, lead us

Friedrich Filitz

3 verses

312 Led like a lamb
(You're alive)

3 verses

Graham Kendrick

© Copyright 1983 Kingsway's Thankyou Music, P.O. Box 75, Eastbourne,
East Sussex, BN23 6NW, UK. Used by permission.

313 Let it be to me

Graham Kendrick

© Copyright 1988 Make Way Music, P.O. Box 263, Croydon, Surrey, CR9 5AP, UK.
International copyright secured. All rights reserved. Used by permission.

314 Let it rain

Joel Pott

© Copyright 1995 Joel Pott.

315 Let me be a sacrifice

Daniel Gardner

© Copyright 1981 Integrity's Hosanna! Music. Administered by Kingsway's
Thankyou Music, P.O. Box 75, Eastbourne, East Sussex, BN23 6NW, UK. Used by permission.

316 Let the righteous sing

Bryn Haworth

2 verses

Bright and rhythmic

© Copyright 1991 Kingsway's Thankyou Music, P.O. Box 75, Eastbourne,
East Sussex, BN23 6NW, UK. Used by permission.

317 Let there be love

Dave Bilbrough

Triumphantly

© Copyright 1979 Kingsway's Thankyou Music, P.O. Box 75, Eastbourne,
East Sussex, BN23 6NW, UK. Used by permission.

318 Let your living water flow

(Living water)

John Watson

4 verses

With a strong beat

© Copyright 1986 Ampelos Music. Administered by CopyCare,
P.O. Box 77, Hailsham, East Sussex, BN27 3EF, UK. Used by permission.

319 Let your love come down

Noel and Tricia Richards

2 verses

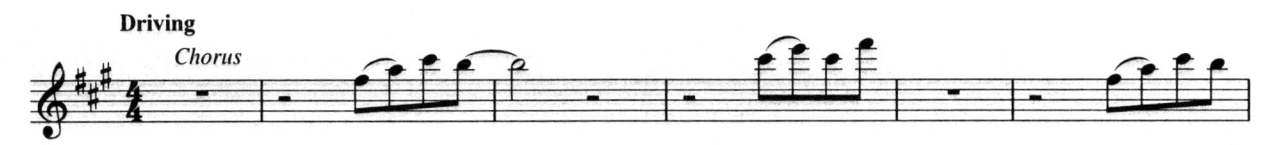

© Copyright 1996 Kingsway's Thankyou Music, P.O. Box 75, Eastbourne,
East Sussex, BN23 6NW, UK. Used by permission.

320 Let your word go forth

Robin Mark

2 verses

© Copyright 1996 Daybreak Music Ltd, Silverdale Road, Eastbourne,
East Sussex, BN20 7AB, UK. Used by permission.

321 Lift up your heads
(O you gates)
Graham Kendrick

3 verses

322 Like a candle flame
(The candle song)
Graham Kendrick

3 verses

323 Living under the shadow of his wing

David Hadden and Bob Silvester

3 verses

With strength

© Copyright 1983 Restoration Music Ltd. Administered by Sovereign Music UK,
P.O. Box 356, Leighton Buzzard, Bedfordshire, LU7 8WP, UK. Used by permission.

324 Lo, he comes with clouds descending

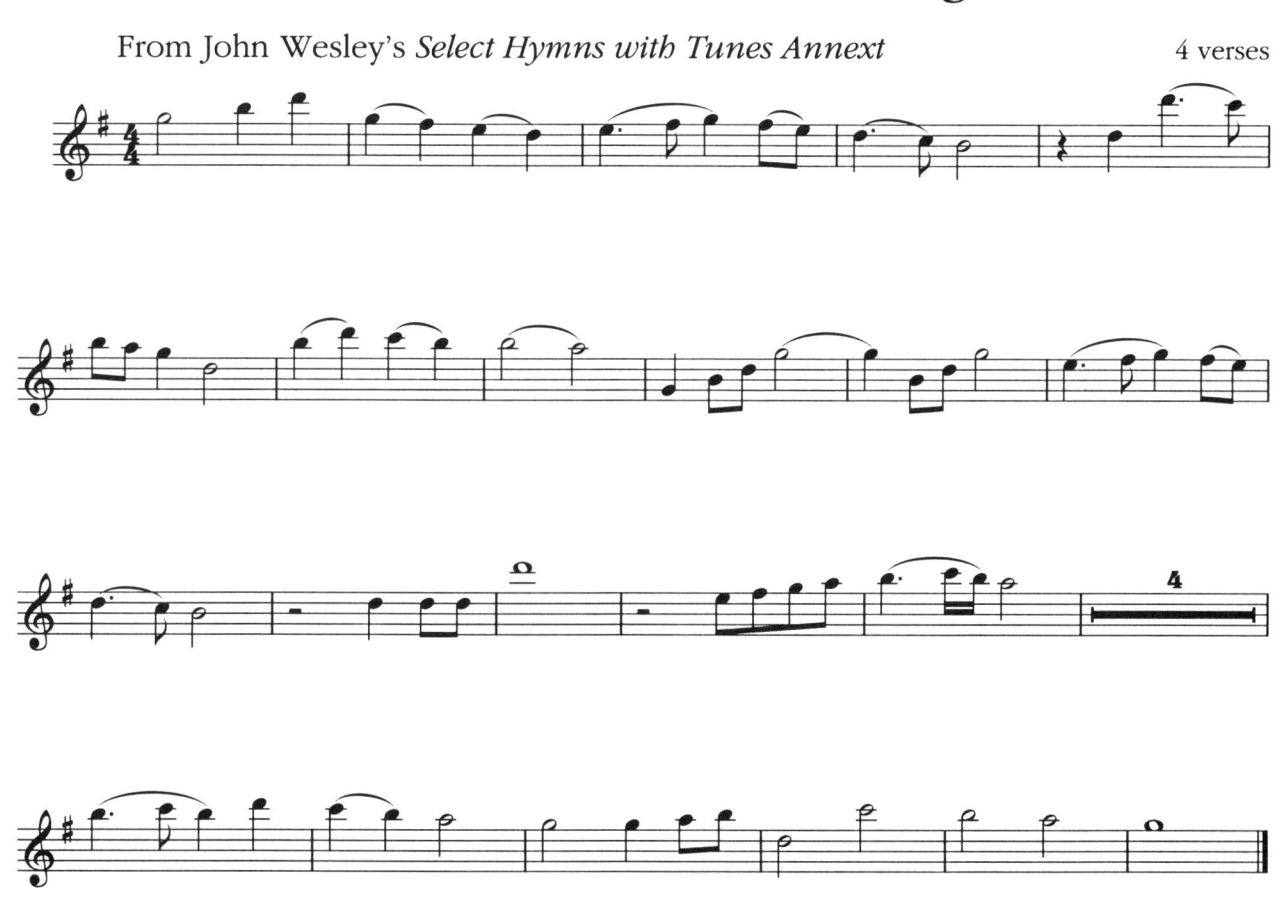

From John Wesley's *Select Hymns with Tunes Annext*

4 verses

325 Look what God has done
(And his love goes on and on)

Graham Kendrick

3 verses

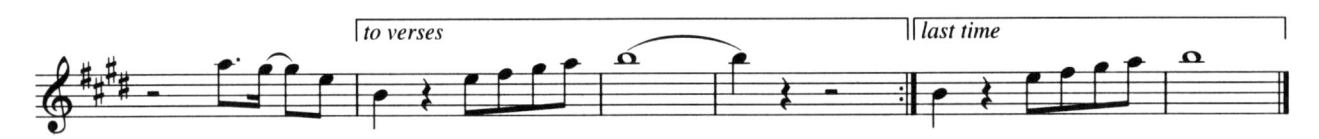

© Copyright 1996 Make Way Music, P.O. Box 263, Croydon, Surrey, CR9 5AP, UK.
International copyright secured. All rights reserved. Used by permission.

326 Look what the Lord has done

Mark David Hanby

© Copyright 1974 Exaltation Music. Administered by Ministry Management Associates,
P.O. Box1248 Decatur, AL 35602-1248, USA. Used by permission.

327 Lord, for the years
(Lord of the years)
Michael Baughen

5 verses

© Copyright Michael Baughen/Jubilate Hymns, 4 Thorne Park Road, Chelston, Torquay, Devon, TQ2 6RX. Used by permission.

328 Lord, have mercy
(Prayer song)
Graham Kendrick

© Copyright 1991 Make Way Music, P.O. Box 263, Croydon, Surrey, CR9 5AP, UK.
International copyright secured. All rights reserved. Used by permission.

329 Lord, I come to you
(Power of your love)
Geoff Bullock

3 verses

© Copyright 1992 Word Music Inc. Administered by CopyCare,
P.O. Box 77, Hailsham, East Sussex, BN27 3EF, UK. Used by permission.

330 Lord, I lift your name on high
(You came from heaven to earth)
Rick Founds

© Copyright 1989 Maranatha! Music. Administered by CopyCare,
P.O. Box 77, Hailsham, East Sussex, BN27 3EF, UK. Used by permission.

331 Lord, my heart cries out
(Glory to the King)

Darlene Zschech

© Copyright 1997 Darlene Zschech/Hillsongs Australia, Administered by Kingsway's Thankyou Music, P.O. Box 75, Eastbourne, East Sussex, BN23 6NW, UK. Used by permission.

332 Lord of lords

Jessy Dixon, Randy Scruggs and John Thompson

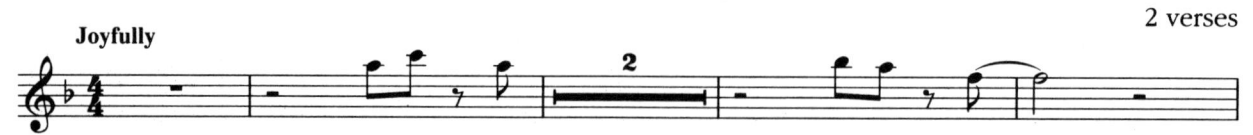

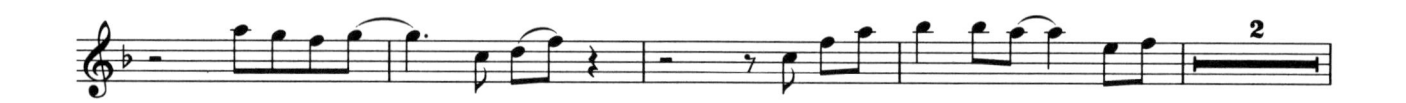

2 verses

Joyfully

© Copyright 1983 Windswept Pacific Music Ltd,
27 Queensdale Place, London, W11 4SQ. Used by permission.

333 Lord of the heavens

Lucy Fisher

© Copyright 1996 Lucy Fisher/Hillsongs Australia. Administered by Kingsway's
Thankyou Music, P.O. Box 75, Eastbourne, East Sussex, BN23 6NW, UK. Used by permission.

334 Lord, prepare me
(Sanctuary)
John Thompson and Randy Scruggs

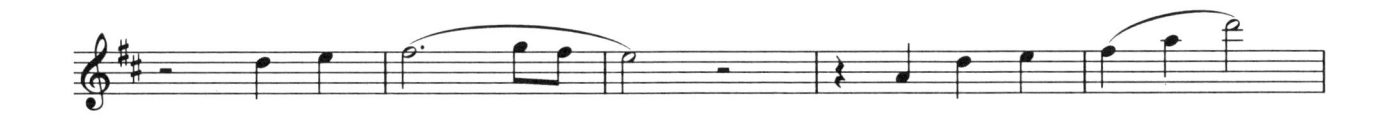

© Copyright 1982 Windswept Pacific Music Ltd,
27 Queensdale Place, London, W11 4SQ. Used by permission.

335 Lord, the light of your love
(Shine, Jesus, shine)

Graham Kendrick

3 verses

Majestic and steady

© Copyright 1987 Make Way Music, P.O. Box 263, Croydon, Surrey, CR9 5AP, UK.
International copyright secured. All rights reserved. Used by permission.

336 Lord, we lift you high

Judy Bailey

© Copyright Ice Music Ltd, Baylet's Plantation,
St. Philip, Barbados, West Indies. Used by permission.

337 Lord, we long for you
(Heal our nation)

Trish Morgan, Ray Goudie, Ian Townend and Dave Bankhead

© Copyright 1986 Kingsway's Thankyou Music, P.O. Box 75, Eastbourne,
East Sussex, BN23 6NW, UK. Used by permission.

338 Lord, we long to see your glory

Richard Lewis

With awe

© Copyright 1997 Kingsway's Thankyou Music, P.O. Box 75, Eastbourne,
East Sussex, BN23 6NW, UK. Used by permission.

339 Lord, you are more precious

Lynn DeShazo

Prayerfully

© Copyright 1982 Integrity's Hosanna! Music. Administered by Kingsway's
Thankyou Music, P.O. Box 75, Eastbourne, East Sussex, BN23 6NW, UK. Used by permission.

340 Lord, you are so precious to me

Graham Kendrick

5 verses

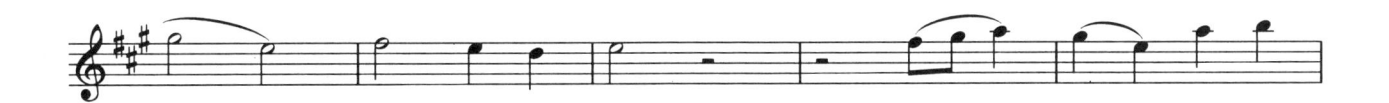

© Copyright 1986 Kingsway's Thankyou Music, P.O. Box 75, Eastbourne,
East Sussex, BN23 6NW, UK. Used by permission.

341 Lord, you have my heart

Martin Smith

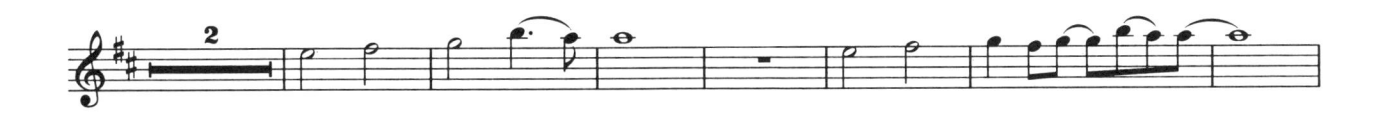

© Copyright 1992 Kingsway's Thankyou Music, P.O. Box 75, Eastbourne,
East Sussex, BN23 6NW, UK. Used by permission.

342 Lord, you put a tongue in my mouth

Ian Smale

With pace

3 verses

© Copyright 1983 Kingsway's Thankyou Music, P.O. Box 75, Eastbourne,
East Sussex, BN23 6NW, UK. Used by permission.

343 Love divine, all loves excelling (Tune 1)

John Stainer

8 verses

343a Love divine, all loves excelling (Tune 2)

William Penfro Rowlands

4 verses

Music © Copyright control (revived 1996)

344 Love of Christ, come now

Graham Kendrick

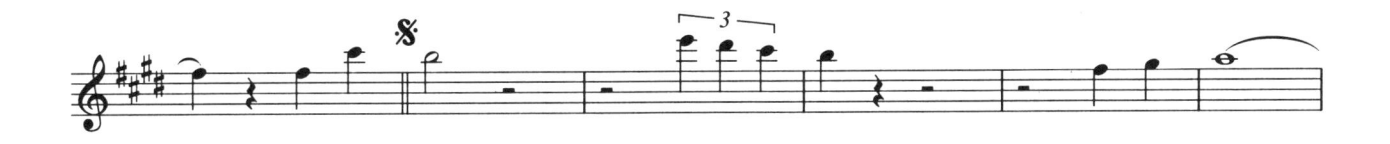

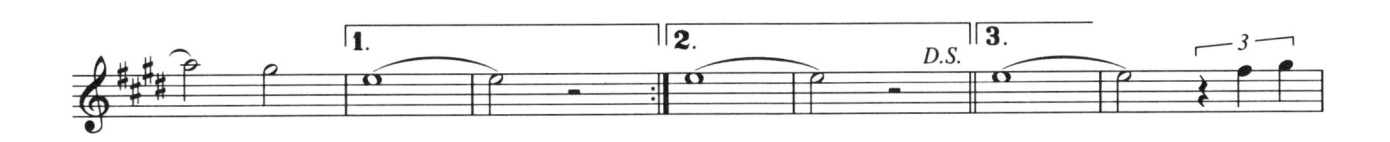

© Copyright 1989 Make Way Music, P.O. Box 263, Croydon, Surrey, CR9 5AP, UK.
International copyright secured. All rights reserved. Used by permission.

345 Low in the grave he lay

Robert Lowry

3 verses

346 Majesty

Jack Hayford

© Copyright 1976 Rocksmith Music. Administered by Leosong Copyright Services Ltd,
Greenland Place, 115/123 Bayham Street, London, NW1 0AR, UK. Used by permission.

347 Make a joyful noise, all ye people
(Worship the Lord)
Edwin Hawkins

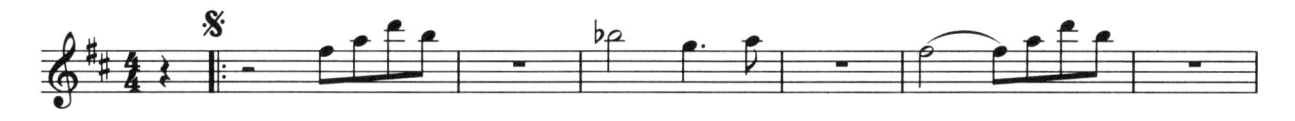

© Copyright 1981 Word Music Inc. Administered by CopyCare,
P.O. Box 77, Hailsham, East Sussex, BN27 3EF, UK. Used by permission.

348 Make me a channel of your peace

Sebastian Temple

3 verses

© Copyright 1967 OCP Publications, 5536 NE Hassalo,
Portland, Oregon 97213 USA. All rights reserved. Used by permission.

349 Make way, make way

Graham Kendrick

4 verses

© Copyright 1986 Kingsway's Thankyou Music, P.O. Box 75, Eastbourne,
East Sussex, BN23 6NW, UK. Used by permission.

350 Man of sorrows

Philipp Bliss

5 verses

351 May our worship be as fragrance
(A living sacrifice)
Chris Bowater

© Copyright 1992 Sovereign Lifestyle Music, P.O. Box 356,
Leighton Buzzard, Bedfordshire, LU7 8WP, UK. Used by permission.

352 May the fragrance
Graham Kendrick

3 verses

Worshipfully

© Copyright 1986 Kingsway's Thankyou Music, P.O. Box 75, Eastbourne,
East Sussex, BN23 6NW, UK. Used by permission.

353 Meekness and majesty
(This is your God)

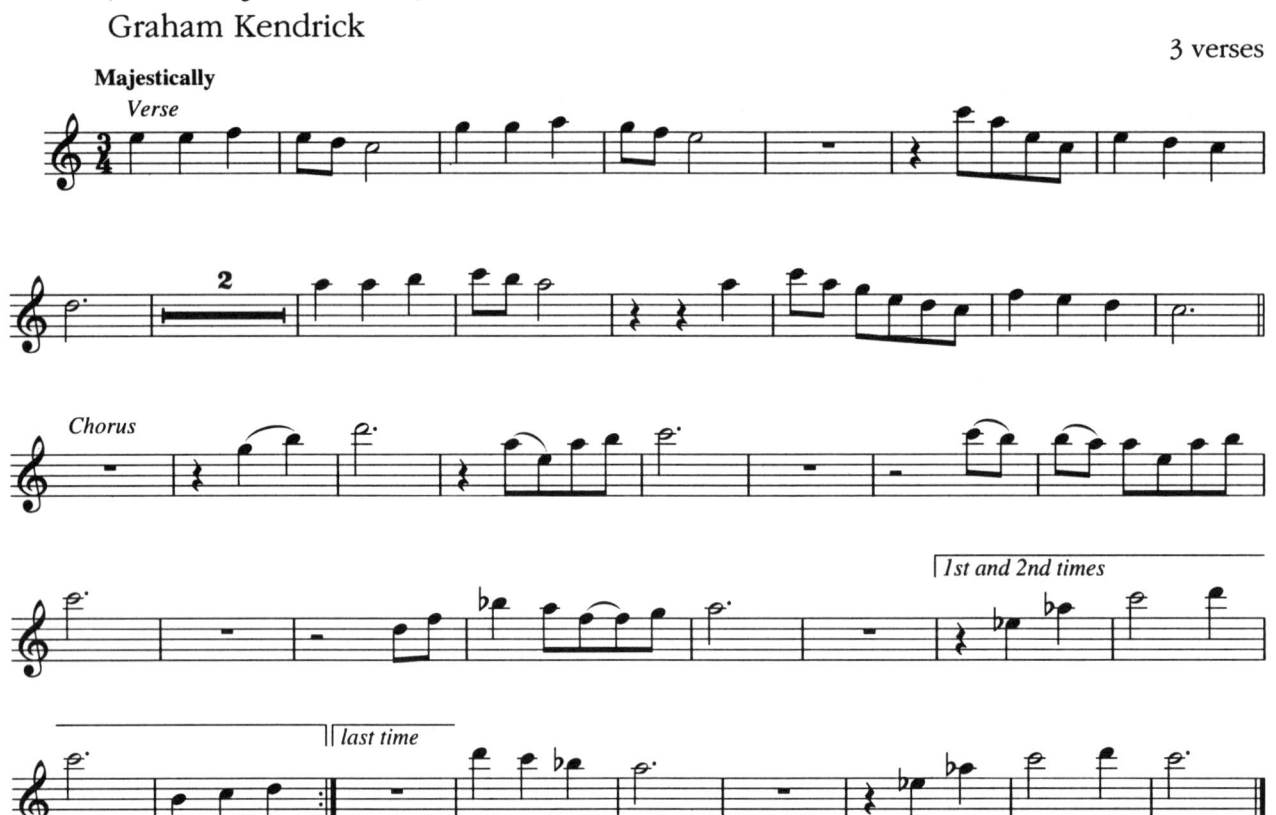

Graham Kendrick

3 verses

Majestically

© Copyright 1986 Kingsway's Thankyou Music, P.O. Box 75, Eastbourne,
East Sussex, BN23 6NW, UK. Used by permission.

354 Men of faith
(Shout to the north)

(Martin Smith)

3 verses

© Copyright 1995 Curious? Music UK. Administered by Kingsway's
Thankyou Music, P.O. Box 75, Eastbourne, East Sussex, BN23 6NW, UK. Used by permission.

355 Mercy is falling

David Ruis

© Copyright 1994 Mercy/Vineyard Publishing/Music Services. Administered by CopyCare,
P.O. Box 77, Hailsham, East Sussex, BN27 3EF, UK. Used by permission.

356 Mighty God

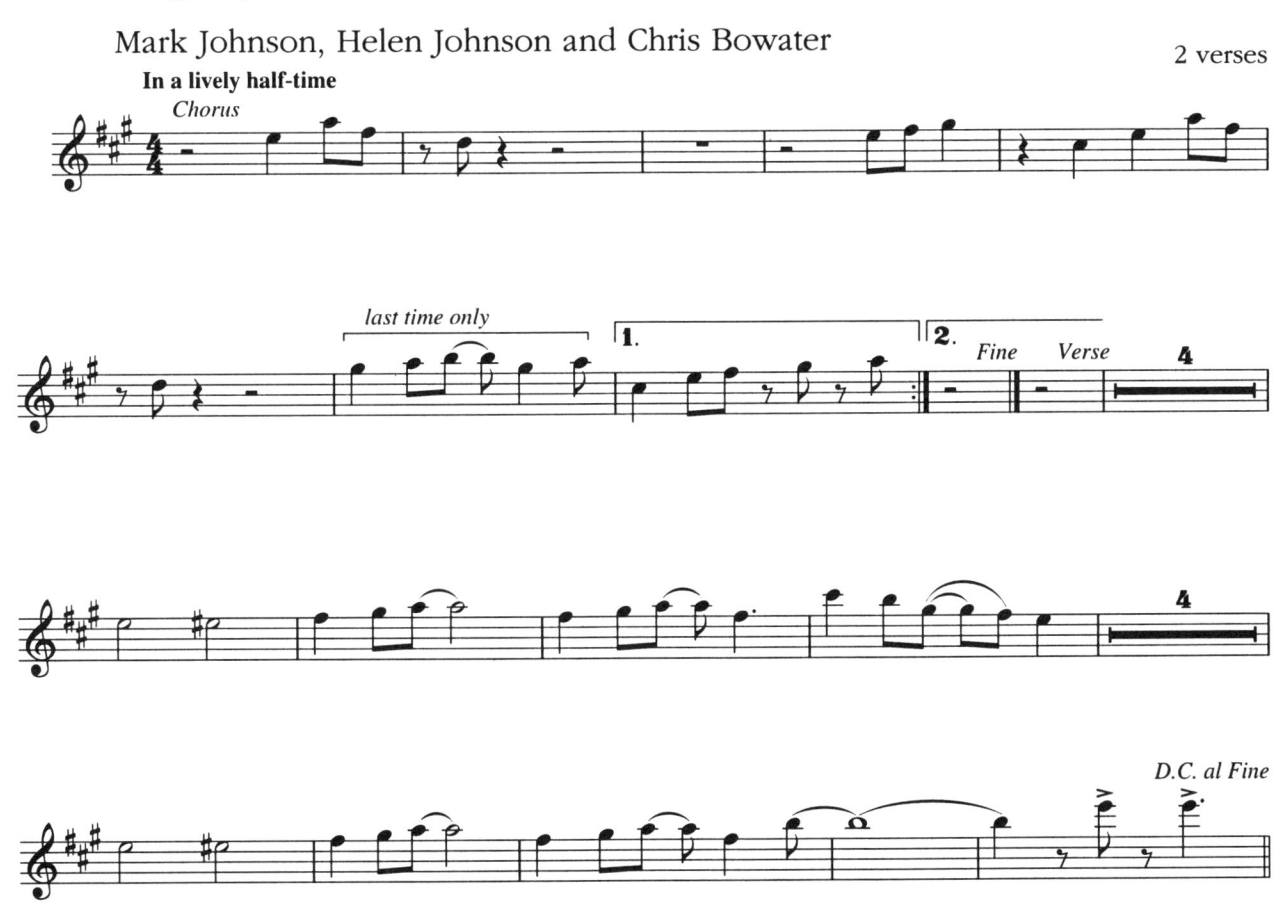

Mark Johnson, Helen Johnson and Chris Bowater

2 verses

© Copyright 1991 Sovereign Lifestyle Music Ltd, P.O. Box 356,
Leighton Buzzard, Bedfordshire, LU7 8WP, UK. Used by permission.

357 Mighty is our God

Eugene Greco, Gerrit Gustafson and Don Moen

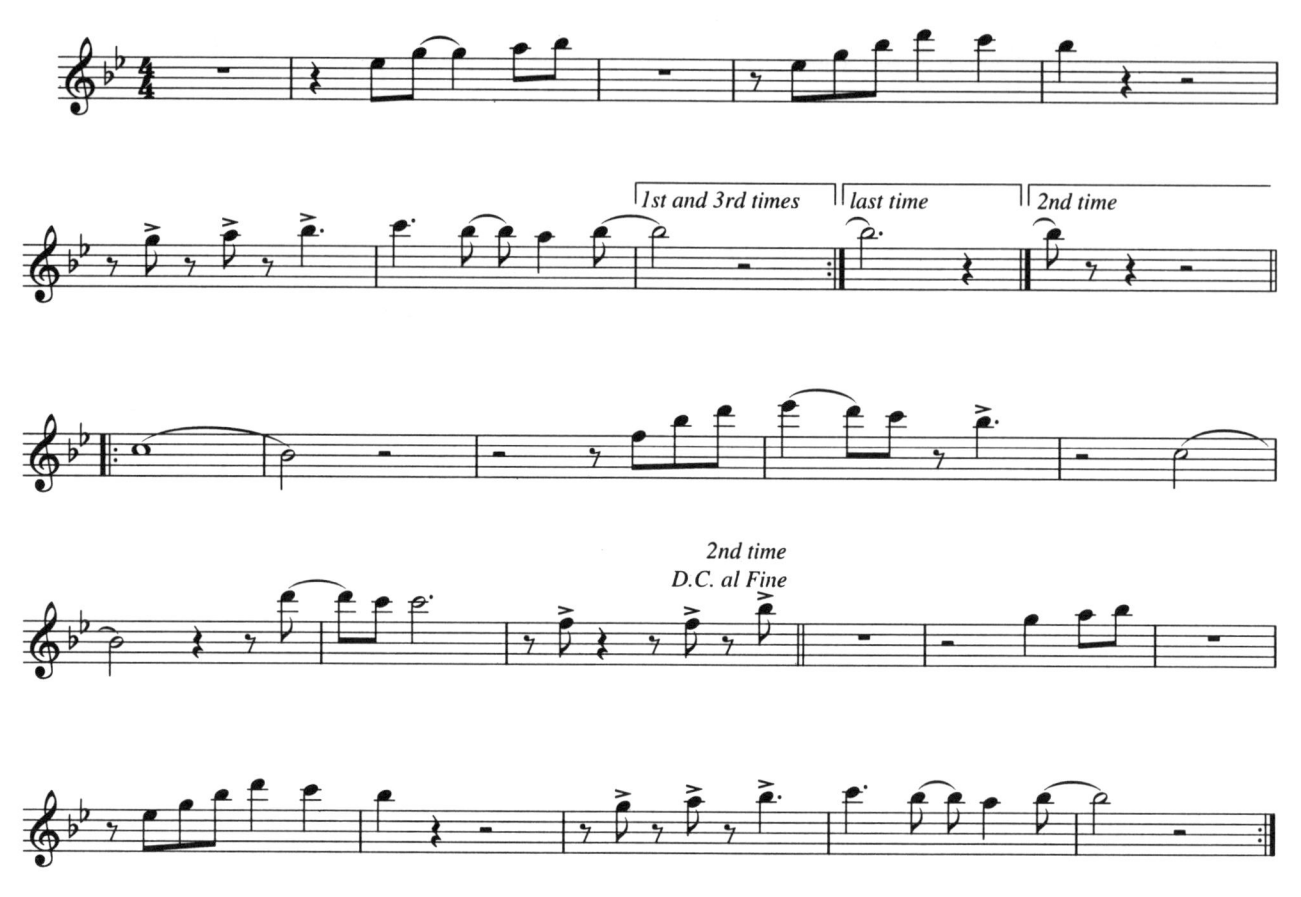

© Copyright 1989 Integrity's Hosanna! Music. Administered by Kingsway's Thankyou Music,
P.O. Box 75, Eastbourne, East Sussex, BN23 6NW, UK. Used by permission.

358 More about Jesus

J.R. Sweney

4 verses

359 More love, more power

Jude del Hierro

360 More of your glory

Lindell Cooley and Bruce Haynes

© Copyright 1987 Mercy/Vineyard Publishing/Music Services. Administered by CopyCare,
P.O. Box 77, Hailsham, East Sussex, BN27 3EF, UK. Used by permission.

© Copyright 1996 Integrity's Hosanna! Music. Administered by Kingsway's Thankyou Music,
P.O. Box 75, Eastbourne, East Sussex, BN23 6NW, UK/Centergy Music. Administered by CopyCare,
P.O. Box 77, Hailsham, East Sussex, BN27 3EF, UK. Used by permission.

361 More than oxygen

Brian Doerksen

3 verses

© Copyright 1995 Mercy/Vineyard Publishing/Music Services. Administered by CopyCare,
P.O. Box 77, Hailsham, East Sussex, BN27 3EF, UK. Used by permission.

362 My first love
(Like a child)

Stuart Townend

3 verses

As a jig

363 My heart is full
(All the glory)
Graham Kendrick

3 verses

© Copyright 1991 Make Way Music, P.O. Box 263, Croydon, Surrey, CR9 5AP, UK.
International copyright secured. All rights reserved. Used by permission.

364 My heart will sing to you
(Great love)
Robin Mark

2 verses

© Copyright 1996 Daybreak Music Ltd, Silverdale Road, Eastbourne,
East Sussex, BN23 6NW, UK. Used by permission.

365 My hope is built (Version 1)
(The Solid Rock)

W.B. Bradbury

4 verses

With life

365a My hope is built (Version 2)
(The Solid Rock)

Traditional

4 verses

Slowly

This arrangement © Copyright 1991 Mercy/Vineyard Publishing/Music Services. Administered by CopyCare, P.O. Box 77, Hailsham, East Sussex, BN27 3EF, UK. Used by permission.

366 My Jesus, I love thee

William R. Featherston and Adoniram J. Gordon

3 verses

© Copyright 1995 Latter Rain Music/Universal Songs. Administered by CopyCare,
P.O. Box 77, Hailsham, East Sussex, BN27 3EF, UK. Used by permission.

367 My Jesus, my Saviour
(Shout to the Lord)

Darlene Zschech

Growing in strength

© Copyright 1993 Darlene Zschech/Hillsongs Australia. Administered by Kingsway's
Thankyou Music, P.O. Box 75, Eastbourne, East Sussex, BN23 6NW, UK. Used by permission.

368 My life is in you, Lord

Daniel Gardner

© Copyright 1986 Integrity's Hosanna! Music. Administered by Kingsway's
Thankyou Music, P.O. Box 75, Eastbourne, East Sussex, BN23 6NW, UK. Used by permission.

369 My lips shall praise you
(Restorer of my soul)

Noel and Tricia Richards — 3 verses

With energy

© Copyright 1991 Kingsway's Thankyou Music, P.O. Box 75, Eastbourne,
East Sussex, BN23 6NW, UK. Used by permission.

370 My Lord, what love is this
(Amazing love)

Graham Kendrick — 3 verses

With strength

© Copyright 1989 Make Way Music, P.O.Box 263, Croydon, Surrey, CR9 5AP, UK.
International copyright secured. All rights reserved. Used by permission.

371 My Spirit rests in you
(Shadow of your wings)

Reuben Morgan

2 verses

© Copyright 1997 Reuben Morgan/Hillsongs Australia. Administered by Kingsway's
Thankyou Music, P.O. Box 75, Eastbourne, East Sussex, BN23 6NW, UK. Used by permission.

372 Nearer, my God, to thee
Lowell Mason

5 verses

373 No one but you, Lord
(Only you)
Andy Park

2 verses

Slowly, with strength

© Copyright 1988 Mercy/Vineyard Publishing/Music Services. Administered by CopyCare,
P.O. Box 77, Hailsham, East Sussex, BN27 3EF, UK. Used by permission.

374 No other name

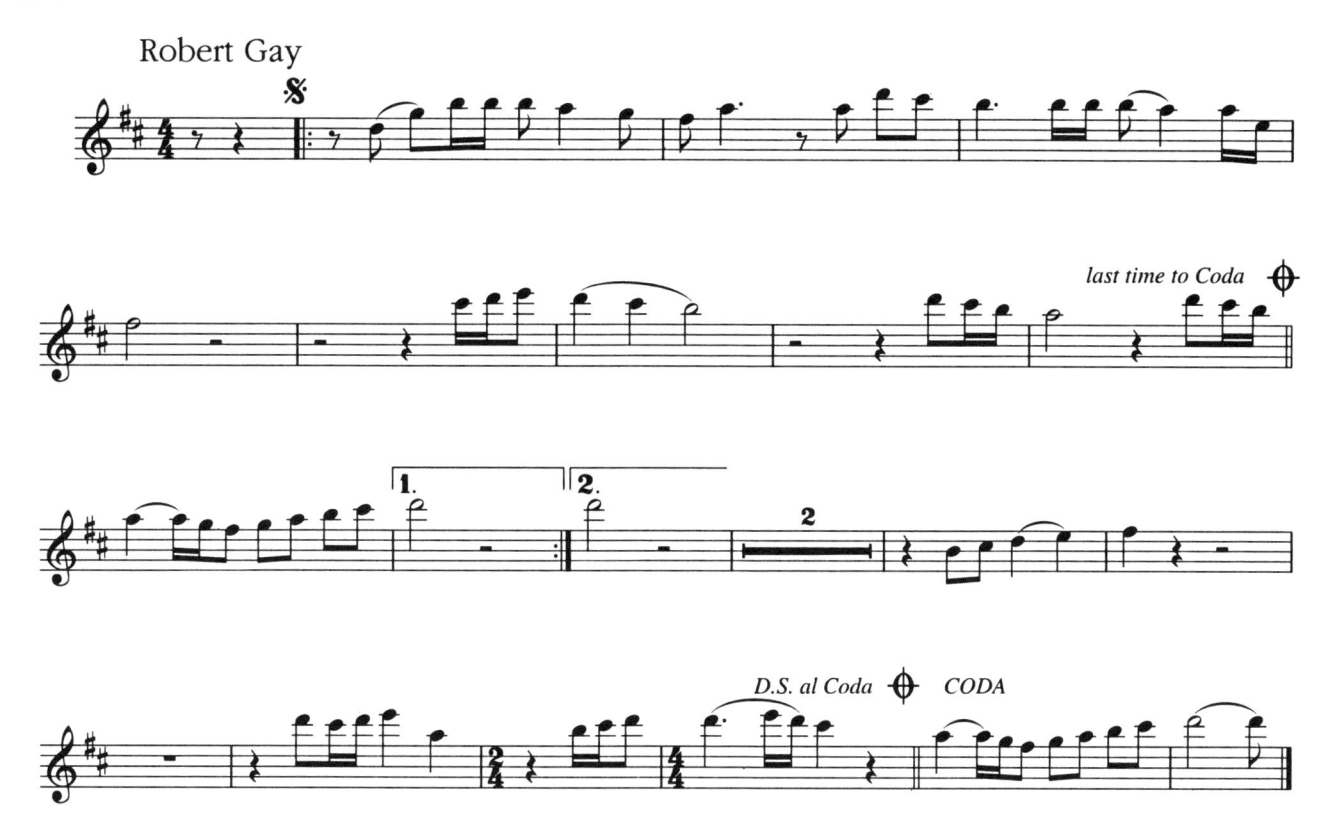

Robert Gay

© Copyright 1988 Integrity's Hosanna! Music. Administered by Kingsway's
Thankyou Music, P.O. Box 75, Eastbourne, East Sussex, BN23 6NW, UK. Used by permission.

375 No scenes of stately majesty

Graham Kendrick

5 verses

© Copyright 1997 Make Way Music,
P.O. Box 263, Croydon, Surrey, CR9 5AP, UK. Used by permission.

376 Not by might

Robin Mark

© Copyright 1996 Daybreak Music, ICC Studios, Silverdale Road, Eastbourne,
East Sussex, BN20 7AB, UK. Used by permission.

377 Nothing shall seperate us

Noel and Tricia Richards

Strong and bright 3 verses

© Copyright 1989 Kingsway's Thankyou Music, P.O. Box 75, Eastbourne,
East Sussex, BN23 6NW, UK. Used by permission.

378 Now unto the King
(Unto the King)

Joey Holder

379 O Breath of life

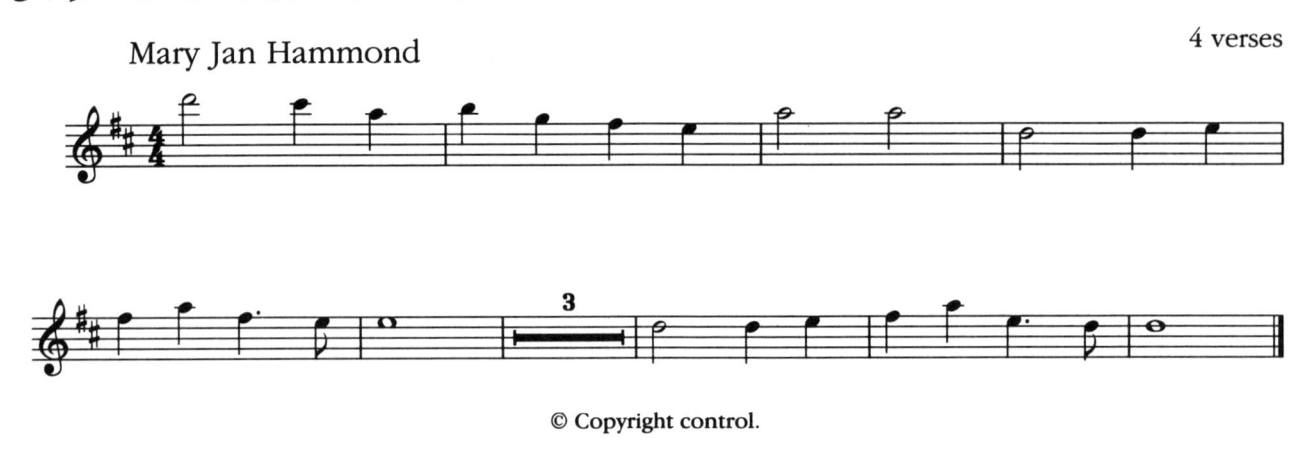

Mary Jan Hammond

4 verses

© Copyright control.

380 O come, all ye faithful

Possibly by John Francis Wade

6 verses

381 O come and join the dance

Graham Kendrick

4 verses

(3rd verse instrumental)

© Copyright 1988 Make Way Music, P.O. Box 263, Croydon, Surrey, CR9 5AP, UK.
International copyright secured. All rights reserved. Used by permission.

382 O Father of the fatherless
(Father me)
Graham Kendrick

4 verses

© Copyright 1992 Make Way Music, P.O. Box 263, Croydon, Surrey, CR9 5AP, UK.
International copyright secured. All rights reserved. Used by permission.

383 O for a thousand tongues to sing

Thomas Jarman

6 verses

384 O give thanks

Graham Kendrick

4 verses

Medium fast, reggae style

© Copyright 1991 Make Way Music, P.O. Box 263, Croydon, Surrey, CR9 5AP, UK.
International copyright secured. All rights reserved. Used by permission.

385 O God, most high
(You have broken the chains)

Jamie Owens-Collins

2 verses

With strength

386 O God of burning, cleansing flame
(Send the fire)

Lex Loizides   4 verses

© Copyright 1994 Kingsway's Thankyou Music, P.O. Box 75, Eastbourne,
East Sussex, BN23 6NW, UK. Used by permission.

387 O happy day

Ron Jones   4 verses

© Copyright Ron Jones.

388 O, heaven is in my heart
(Heaven is in my heart)
Graham Kendrick

3 verses

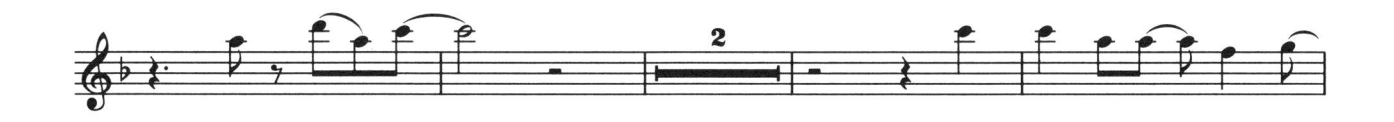

389 Oh, I was made for this
(I was made for this)

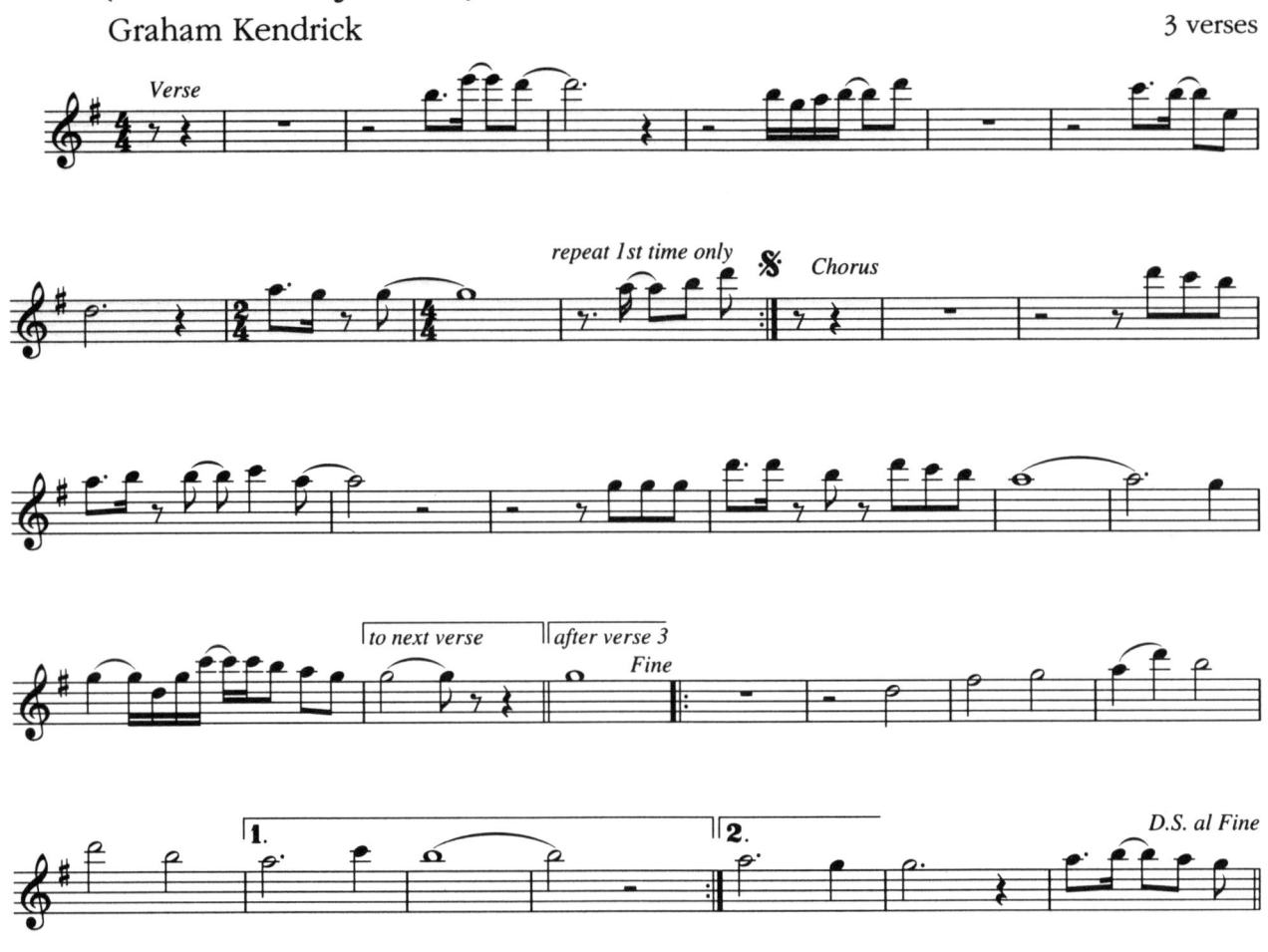

Graham Kendrick

3 verses

390 Oh, lead me

Martin Smith

© Copyright 1994 Curious? Music UK. Administered by Kingsway's Thankyou Music,
P.O. Box 75, Eastbourne, East Sussex, BN23 6NW, UK. (Worldwide) Used by permission.

391 O Jesus, I have promised

Geoffrey Beaumont

5 verses

© Copyright 1960 Josef Weinberger Ltd, 12-14 Mortimer Street, London, W1N 7RD.
Used by permission.

392 O let the Son of God enfold you
(Spirit song)

John Wimber

2 verses

© Copyright 1995 Mercy/Vineyard Publishing/Music Services. Administered by CopyCare,
P.O. Box 77, Hailsham, East Sussex, BN27 3EF, UK. Used by permission.

393 O little town of Bethlehem

4 verses

Traditional English melody collected by Ralph Vaughan Williams

© Copyright Oxford University Press, 70 Baker Street, London, W1M 1DJ.
Used by permission from the *English Hymnal*

394 O Lord, hear my prayer

Jacques Berthier

© Copyright Ateliers et Presses de Taizé.
Taizé-Communauté, F-71250, France. Used by permission.

395 O Lord, how majestic is your name
(How majestic)

Ben Lindquist and Don Moen

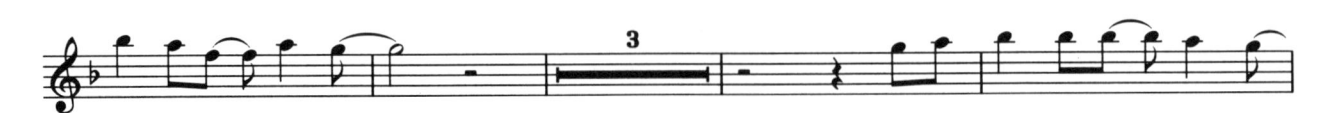

© Copyright 1990 Integrity's Hosanna! Music. Administered by Kingsway's
Thankyou Music, P.O. Box 75, Eastbourne, East Sussex, BN23 6NW, UK. Used by permission.

396 O Lord, my God
(How great thou art)

Swedish folk melody collected by Stuart K. Hine

4 verses

© Copyright 1953 Stuart K. Hine. Administered by Kingsway's Thankyou Music, P.O. Box 75, Eastbourne, East Sussex, BN23 6NW, UK. Worldwide (excl. Canada & USA.) Used by permission.

397 O Lord, my heart is not proud

Margaret Rizza

Calm

to repeat ad lib. | *last time*

© Copyright 1997 Kevin Mayhew Ltd.

398 O Lord our God
(We will magnify)

Philip Lawson Johnson

3 verses

Flowing

Verse

Chorus

© Copyright 1982 Kingsway's Thankyou Music, P.O. Box 75, Eastbourne,
East Sussex, BN23 6NW, UK. Used by permission.

399 O Lord, the clouds are gathering

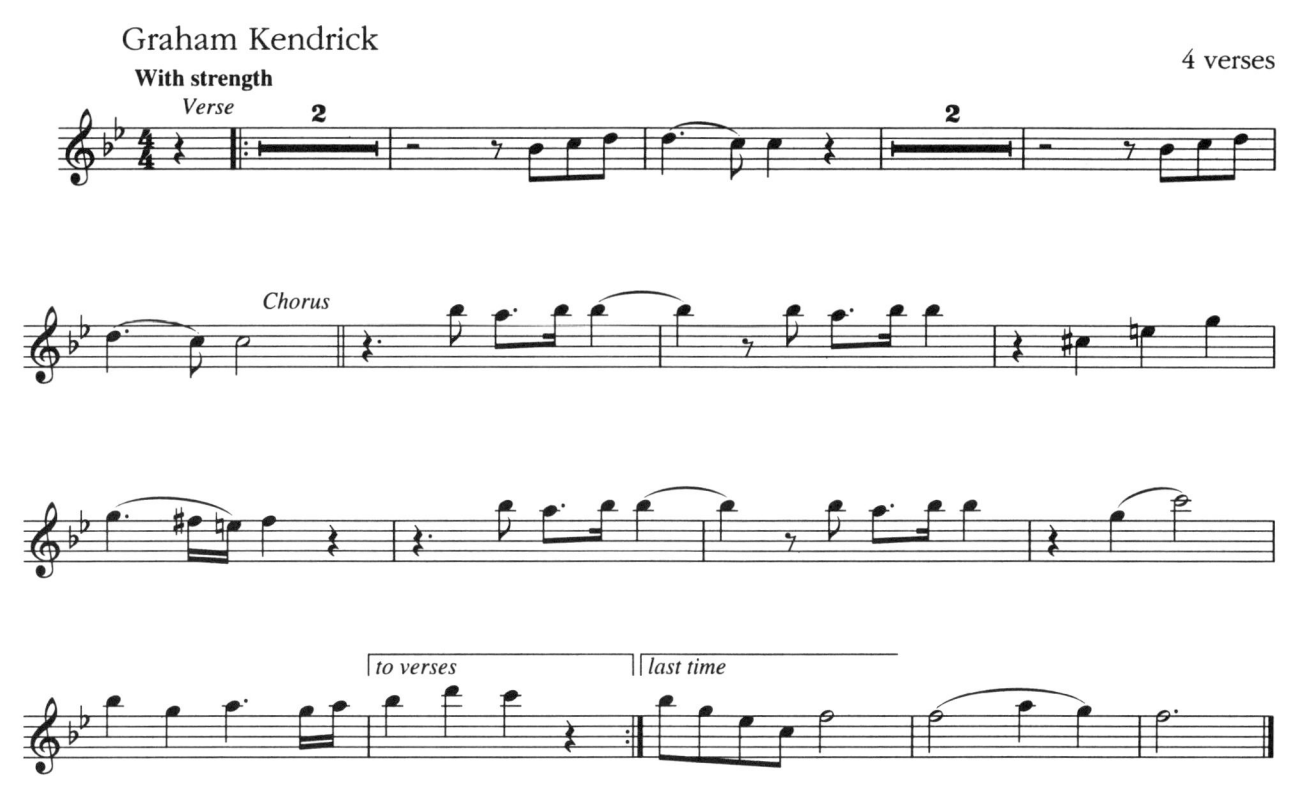

Graham Kendrick

4 verses

With strength

© Copyright 1987 Make Way Music, P.O. Box 263, Croydon, Surrey, CR9 5AP, UK.
International copyright secured. All rights reserved. Used by permission.

400 O Lord, you lead me
(Have faith in God)

Geoff Bullock

2 verses

© Copyright 1993 Word Music Inc. Administered by CopyCare,
P.O. Box 77, Hailsham, East Sussex, BN27 3EF, UK. Used by permission.